NOW HIRING: FILM

by Michael Serrian

Crestwood House
New York

Maxwell Macmillan Canada
Toronto

Maxwell Macmillan International
New York   Oxford   Singapore   Sydney

Crestwood House
Macmillan Publishing Company
866 Third Avenue
New York, NY 10022

Maxwell Macmillan Canada, Inc.
1200 Eglinton Avenue East
Suite 200
Don Mills, Ontario M3C 3N1

Produced by Twelfth House Productions
Designed by R Studio T
photo credits:
cover: man with mask, courtesy of Neil Martz, other photos by Brian Vaughan
Brian Vaughan: 5, 20, 22, 26, 27, 29, 31, 34, 36
Laura McLean: 8
courtesy of Bill Lister: 11, 13
courtesy of Dick Smith: 16
courtesy of Neil Martz: 18

Macmillan Publishing Company is part of the Maxwell Communication Group of Companies.

First Edition

Printed in the United States of America

10   9   8   7   6   5   4   3   2   1

Library of Congress Cataloging-in-Publication Data

Serrian, Michael.
    Film / by Michael Serrian.—1st ed.
        p.   cm.—(Now hiring)
    Includes index.
    Summary: Surveys the different types of jobs available in the film
industry, from driver to sound recordist, and discusses their duties
and qualifications.
    ISBN 0-89686-784-6
    1. Motion picture industry—Vocational guidance—Juvenile
literature.   2. Film—Job descriptions—Juvenile Literature.
[1. Motion picture industry.   2. Vocational guidance.]
I. Title.   II. Series: Now hiring.
PN1995.9.P75S47   1994
791.43'02'93—dc20   93–2018

0-382-24748-5 (pbk.)

CONTENTS

THIS BUSINESS OF FILM

Everybody loves going to the movies. It's exciting to buy your ticket and find a seat in the dimly lit theater. And when the lights are turned off, the images on the big screen sweep you away to another world. Movies are magic!

When you go to a movie, you usually know who some of the actors are. And you might know who directed the film. Most people are familiar with the names of superstars like Arnold Schwarzenegger or directors like Steven Spielberg. But you probably have never heard of any of the people who work behind the scenes to make that movie happen.

For every famous actor, there are hundreds of people working to create movies. These people include electricians, makeup artists, film editors, sound recordists, drivers, and more. And there could be a creative or technical job in the film industry waiting for you!

What does it take to get a job in film? A lot of hard work and persistence. A job is not just handed to you because you're looking for work. You have to prove yourself. The studios are looking for hardworking people who share their passion for movies.

The many people interviewed in this book learned their specific craft on the job. They came in as a **gofer** or **production assistant** and watched what was going on around them. Then they used their knowledge to get the job of their dreams.

Most of the workers in Hollywood are **union** employees. The unions negotiate wages and benefits for their members with the major studios. Most of the unions are closed to newcomers. But if you're persistent, you'll eventually get into one.

It might take years for you to get your break in the film industry. The people in this book are the lucky ones. They stuck it out, learning their craft over the years.

4

In the following pages, you'll meet men and women who found jobs in film that make them proud. They're part of teams that create major motion pictures. Check out their experiences, their insights, their mistakes, and their advice. Maybe you'll find yourself sharing their feelings, their joy, and their love for making movies.

Hundreds of people work on a film behind the scenes before it is released.

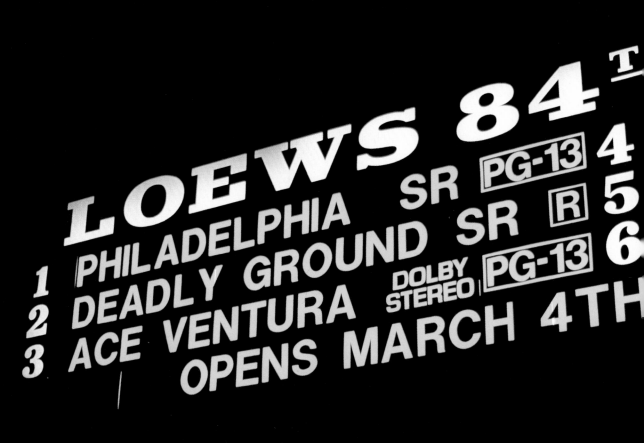

TEAMSTER DRIVER

Nuts and Bolts of the Job

You're driving on the Los Angeles Freeway, trying to beat the traffic. Suddenly, your pager goes off—"CHIRP-CHIRP." The sound gets more and more intense until you hit the button. You have to call the dispatch office, and there's not a moment to spare. When you get beeped, it means the office needs something done, fast.

Greg knows all about getting beeped. He's been a **teamster driver** for seven years. It's his job to pick up and deliver items to and from different places. "I'm sent to take something from one point to another point. Things like film reels, scripts, sound tracks, and contracts. Sometimes I need to drop stuff off at a movie location. Those are the fun jobs," says Greg.

Greg spends most of his time behind the wheel of his car. He's usually picking something up, dropping something off, or both. "I'm always on the run," Greg says. Besides his car, Greg's tools are a pager (or beeper) and two-way radio (like a walkie-talkie). The dispatch office uses these machines to reach Greg when he's on the road. Even when he's delivering something, he might be getting other assignments. "I'm always on call. Everything is a rush," he explains.

RELATED JOBS:
Gaffer
Production
assistant

"The first thing I do in the morning is check in at the dispatch office on the main lot of the studio," Greg explains. The dispatch office assigns Greg his first runs for that day. Then he hits the road.

When Greg drops something off, someone has to sign for the item. Information about the package, like the time and place it was delivered, is recorded in a log book, along with the recipient's signature.

Once Greg completes his first runs, he calls in to get more assignments. "Or I drive back to the studio to pick up more runs," Greg says.

Greg has to do his runs quickly and efficiently. "There's a lot of weight on my shoulders to do everything as fast as possible," he says. If there's a problem or something is late, the driver is responsible. "Problems are always the driver's fault," Greg complains. That's why Greg tries to deliver packages as fast as he can.

"Last week I had one of those days," Greg relates. "It was a rainy day, and I had a run from downtown Los Angeles to Orange County and back. Man, it was three, four hours and very intense," he says. Unfortunately, the dispatch office keeps track of how many runs a driver makes each day and not the length of each run. "That was considered a light day for me," Greg says.

Greg likes being a driver but admits that the job has its drawbacks. "It can be hard to deal with people waiting for something on the other end." And he adds that "the stress of driving in heavy traffic and wet weather can be tough to handle." Plus, there's vehicle maintenance. He's got to make sure that his car runs well.

Eventually, Greg hopes to move up to the position of **location driver**. He or she moves sets, props, and lighting equipment to the **location**, the place away from the studio, where a film is shot. Location drivers also provide transportation for the **talent**. "Driv-

"I'M ALWAYS ON THE RUN."

A teamster driver plans a route with her dispatcher.

ing movie stars around would be pretty exciting," says Greg.

Greg jokes that the best part of his job is "five o'clock, when I get off." Actually, Greg enjoys meeting other people in the film industry. "The nicest people are the sound people. They seem to be the coolest for some reason. And most of the editors," he says.

Have You Got What It Takes?

A teamster driver is always on the go. You're under pressure to get things where they need to be. You've got to know your way around the city. You need to be able to beat traffic. And you have to make sure that all the information about a delivery is recorded correctly.

8

Greg says he got his job because he was in the right place at the right time. "I was pretty lucky. My roommate's friend was looking for a messenger at her company. She offered the job to him, but he wasn't interested. When he suggested me, she hired me on the spot. Normally they want someone with at least one year's experience as a messenger," he explains.

The job was a break for Greg in another way, too. It helped him get into the driver's union. "It can be really hard to get into the union. But the union came to *me* and asked if I wanted to join. A group of us at the messenger service got in at the same time. It was the perfect chance to get it, so we went for it," he says.

A good driver should be "very patient and efficient," Greg says. You can't freak out when you're trying to get somewhere and traffic is holding you up. "Sometimes there's nothing you can do about it," Greg says. But you also need to know how to get around traffic when you can. If there's an alternate route, you should know about it. A driver should also be reliable. The people you work with need to know that you're there whenever they need you.

Interested? It's a good idea to get some job experience. Ask your parents or your school guidance counselor or other adults if they know of any businesses that are looking for general help around the office.

Experience as a messenger will also be helpful. If you live in a large city, look in the yellow pages under "delivery services." Even if you don't have a car, you can deliver packages on a bike.

Once you get some messenger or delivery experience, it will be easier to get a job as a driver. (If you need to get a driver's license, you should inquire about driver's ed courses in your school or community.) Be prepared to work outside the film industry for a while. As Greg mentions, most studios look for messengers with at least one year's experience. But don't let that stop you! There's a spot behind the wheel waiting for you!

Nuts and Bolts of the Job

The **director of photography** (DP) on a major motion picture asks you to set up the lights for a daylight scene. What lights would you use? And where would you put them?

Enter **gaffer** Tony. Tony is the chief electrical lighting technician. That means he's in charge of all the electricity on the set.

Tony works closely with the director of photography. Before the shooting of a film begins, Tony reads the script. Then he meets with the DP to talk about what kinds of lights and camera angles will be used in the film. "I have to find out what kind of effect the DP wants in each scene. Together we create all the lighting setups," Tony explains.

Tony also works with **grips**. Grips are responsible for putting up the sets and for rigging (constructing) the equipment on the set. They also take care of camera movement. The **key grip** is the grip in charge. Tony and the key grip work very closely.

Basically, Tony and the key grip do whatever is necessary to set up lights the way the DP wants them. "After I find out what the DP wants, the key grip and I decide what lights we will use. We also talk about where the lights will go and how they will be balanced," he says.

Next, Tony prepares a list of all electrical equipment required for a specific film. Then he takes his list to several rental equipment companies. They bid on the job by telling Tony how much they will charge for the use of the equipment. After Tony has several bids, he decides which company to use.

"Once I have the equipment, I talk over the setups with the **best boy**." The best boy is Tony's right-hand person—the second in command.

Gaffer Bill Lister operates the lights from an elevated platform.

Rigging and operating lights isn't easy. "Lighting gear is really heavy, a gut buster," Tony moans. "The crew has to string these heavy lamps along the beams above the stages. It's tough and dangerous."

Tony likes to do as much prep work as he can before each shoot. "You really should scout the shoot locations prior to production," Tony recommends. "You don't want any surprises." Tony also tries to **prerig** as much as possible. Prerigging means laying down cable everywhere you think lights might be used. That way, you're one step ahead.

Since Tony works for small, independent production companies, he isn't always able to scout locations or prerig. "Set 'em up and shoot, set 'em up and shoot. Cheapie films are like TV shows. Real down and dirty," he explains.

RELATED JOBS:
Grip
Key grip
Set carpenter
Best boy

Still, Tony does everything he can to make things easier for his crew. "Working nonunion, you have to look out for your crew. That's part of my job, too," Tony explains. He negotiates for overtime compensation for himself and his crew. He wants to make sure that everyone gets a fair deal.

Tony says that it's important that the gaffer gets along with the DP. "If I don't like the DP, I don't do the show," Tony says. "When you work with a great DP, then your job is a pleasure," he says. "If there's common respect between you, then you have it made."

Have You Got What It Takes?

A gaffer is in charge of electricity on the set. You have to rent equipment. You have to make sure everything is set up properly. And you're responsible for safety. Sound like a lot to handle? It is!

Tony had the makings of a gaffer from early on. He liked to work with his hands. And, as he tells us, "I was always a guy who liked to work out. I was really into phys ed back in high school."

Also, Tony's father was an electrician. "My interest in electronics came from my dad. I used to tag along with him when he went out on jobs. I'd hold his tools and stuff," Tony remembers.

Tony decided he wanted to get into film when he was a teenager. After high school he got a job in a small, independent studio. He lugged around big equipment such as lights and generators.

After working as a grunt for a while, Tony became a **lamp operator**. He rigged and operated lights. Rigging lights can get a little crazy. "I've been hanging above the set, rigging a 10K light," Tony says. A 10K light is a 10,000 watt light bulb.

"YOU HAVE TO GET IN THERE, SET UP, AND SHOOT."

Tony eventually worked his way up to best boy, then gaffer. "I love being a gaffer," Tony smiles, "I light up your life!"

It's important for a gaffer to work well with people. "You have to get in there, set up, and shoot," Tony says. "And to do that, you have to cooperate with the people around you." As the person in charge of electricity, the gaffer makes sure all the lights and cameras work properly. And that takes teamwork.

A gaffer also needs to be in good shape. Sometimes it's necessary to pitch in with your crew and physically handle the heavy equipment.If you're interested in becoming a gaffer, take shop class. And learn about electricity and wiring. If you know someone who's handy, see what you can learn from him or her. Or get your hands on some books about electricity.

You might also get involved in school or community theater. It's not exactly the same as film, but it will familiarize you with lights and electricity.

Tony suggests you look for grunt work, too. If you live in a large city, contact local studios. "Offer to work for free for a week or so. Get your foot in the door," Tony recommends. "The rest is up to you. Work hard and be pleasant and maybe they'll keep you around longer. And if you're really good, maybe they'll even pay you!"

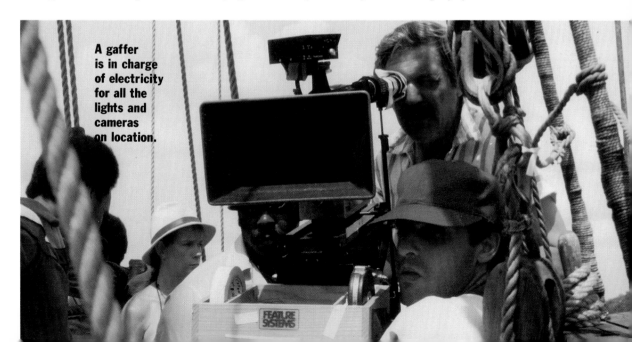

A gaffer is in charge of electricity for all the lights and cameras on location.

SPECIAL EFFECTS MAKEUP ARTIST

Nuts and Bolts of the Job

Your favorite actor is on the screen, looking up at the full moon. Suddenly, hair begins sprouting on his face and body. He howls as his clothes begin to shed from his growing, beast-like body. In mere seconds, he transforms into a raging werewolf!

Who makes this transformation seem all too real? Who's responsible for that incredible makeup?

It's the work of **special effects makeup artists** like Chris. Chris specializes in making monsters. She uses foam latex, foam urethane plastic, plaster, dental materials, and lots of imagination to do her job.

Chris works closely with the director to help realize his or her vision of the monster she'll create. "I create monsters based on the director's ideas," she says. "But sometimes the director doesn't know exactly what he or she wants. That's when I use my imagination and come up with something on my own," she says.

RELATED JOBS:
Makeup assistant
Special effects coordinator
Creature designer

After Chris gets an idea of what the director wants, she does some preliminary drawings. If the director likes her sketches, she starts creating!

"I usually sit the actor down and make a model of his or her face. I might also need to make a cast of other body parts. It depends on what will be shown on camera," she explains.

To make a model, Chris applies plaster to the actor's face. After the plaster dries, Chris removes it in one piece. Now she has a mold, which she fills with more plaster. When this plaster dries, it forms a perfect impression of the actor's face.

With the model of the actor's face in hand, Chris can get to work. She usually makes a mask of latex that fits over the model. If she's making a werewolf, Chris will paint the mask the color of a wolf and add hair. If she's making a deformed human face, she might apply pieces of foam latex to the mask. Foam latex is soft, so it allows the actor to move freely under the mask. It also allows the actor's dramatic expression to be seen on camera.

When it's time for filming, Chris puts the mask on the actor. "I slip on the headpiece and apply additional makeup. The makeup has to be applied carefully, because it must look realistic. The audience shouldn't be able to tell where the real person ends and the monster begins," says Chris. She might also have to put finishing touches on the mask itself.

Even after the mask has been created, making the actor look like a real monster takes a lot of time and effort. "Some makeup sessions run three to four hours," Chris says. That's not easy for Chris or the actor! She also has to worry about skin reactions. "Some actors break out in hives or rashes from the makeup. Then you have to seek out an alternative," explains Chris.

One horror movie Chris worked on featured a zombie. "I came up with a pretty unique design. It was different from the normal *Night of the Living Dead* kind. I was really proud of the concept."

But when Chris showed her design to the director, he said it was terrible. "I was crushed. But I had to swallow my pride and figure out a new concept. When the director didn't like that one, he

"SOME MAKEUP SESSIONS RUN THREE TO FOUR HOURS."

Dick Smith, a special effects makeup artist, creates a mask for the cult film *The Hunger*.

decided to go back to the first one. It worked out in my favor. But it wasn't easy," Chris tells us.

Chris loves working with special effects makeup. "It's fun to create monsters and creatures from scratch," Chris says. "But it's tough work. During a shoot, you're working around the clock. Sometimes I'm lucky if I get two or three hours sleep. It's pretty intense. That's why I take months off between movies."

Most "monster makers" in the movie business are men. Being a woman in a mostly male line of work is challenging. "Little boys grow up with monster movies and comic books more than little girls do," Chris explains. "They're exposed to those fantasy elements earlier and have more inspiration to draw from. But I'm catching up!"

Have You Got What It Takes?

Making monsters is fun! You use your imagination. You work with all kinds of funky materials. But, as Chris points out, it's not always easy to come up with a design that the director likes.

Chris got her start doing makeup in high school. "I had this part-time job at a cosmetics counter in a department store. I learned how to apply makeup from a woman who worked at Revlon," she says.

While working part-time at the cosmetics counter, Chris got involved doing makeup for school plays. She did all the makeup for the performers. "It was neat," Chris says. "I really learned a lot about different stage makeups and how to apply them."

It wasn't long before Chris decided that she wanted to do makeup for movies. Since she lived in Los Angeles, she was already in the right place. "I took a chance and got in touch with a few major studios. But they wouldn't hire me because I wasn't in the union. When I asked how I could get into the union, they said I had to get a professional movie job. But *how*? I couldn't get hired without a union card. It was nuts," Chris remembers.

So Chris got in touch with **independent production companies**. People who work on films for independent production companies don't have to be union members. "I managed to talk my way into being a **makeup assistant** on a biker movie. I helped the makeup artist, doing whatever needed to be done. Most of the makeup was bruises, fake beer bellies, and beards!"

Luckily for Chris, one thing led to another. After a while, she got a job working on a horror film. Chris helped create and do the makeup for the monster. "I had a ball. It was tough work, but it was fun," she tells us.

Chris is still working for independent movie companies on horror, science fiction, and biking films. "I still don't have my union card, but I'm making a very good living at doing what I do best—creating monsters!" she says.

17

A special effects makeup artist should be creative. You have to be good at working with your hands. And you must be patient. You might have to spend hours making up a face—it has to be just right.

It's also important that you have an easygoing personality. Actors should be comfortable around you, because you'll be working closely with them. And sometimes they have to sit still for hours.

If you want to do special effects makeup, get a job selling cosmetics, as Chris did. Once you learn the basics, offer to do makeup for school and community theaters. Or just buy some stage makeup and get your friends to sit still while you go crazy! The important thing is that you practice your craft. The more experience you have, the zanier you can get!

A special effects makeup artist makes adjustments to an actor's mask on the set.

ASSISTANT FILM EDITOR

Nuts and Bolts of the Job

On the screen, a car races down a dark country road. First you see the bright headlights piercing the darkness. Then you notice the driver's face, his eyes straining to see the pavement. Cut back to the dark, eerie road. Suddenly a person steps out in front of the car. The driver brakes hard...

Who helps cut these shots together? Who makes sure they flow together seamlessly?

Assistant film editors like Barbara do. She has worked at Walt Disney Pictures on *The Little Mermaid, The Prince and the Pauper,* and *Aladdin*. These films use the technique of **animation**. Animated movies feature drawn characters that are brought to life with the magic of moviemaking!

As an assistant film editor, Barbara must get the film ready for the **film editor** to work with. "Basically, I'm there to assist the film editor and keep track of everything," Barbara relays.

While the animated characters in the film are being created, the sound is recorded in a studio. "Dialogue is recorded in sections, and each section is recorded several times," Barbara explains. Every time a section is recorded, it is called a take. The director chooses two or three takes—the takes he or she thinks are the best—from each section. These are called **select takes**.

One of Barbara's most important tasks is to build **select rolls**—rolls of sound film that contain the select takes. "I have to sift through all the sound footage and find the select takes. Then I cut them and put them all together, adding or cutting footage so that they sound fairly smooth," she explains.

"SOME FILMS REQUIRE A LOT OF OVERTIME."

While she works, Barbara keeps track of *everything*. "I log everything in. And I keep track of where everything comes from, like what sound track roll and, later, when we add the pictures, what picture roll," Barbara says. This is important, because Barbara and the film editor might want to go back to an original roll when they're cutting the film.

Next, Barbara codes the picture and the track. She uses a **coding machine**, which stamps matching numbers at regular intervals on the film. Coding the film allows the editor to cut the film and still keep track of what is what. Once the film has been coded, Barbara logs everything into a book that lists the code numbers.

As the editor works, Barbara keeps track of the **trims** he or she makes. Trims are pieces of takes that are left over after a portion of

An assistant film editor works on a flatbed.

that take has been cut out. And sometimes she has to go back and find additional takes. "And I might have to deal with film labs if there are any problems," Barbara tells us. If a film gets torn, Barbara calls the lab for a reprint.

Another one of Barbara's tasks is to create head and tail **leaders**. Leaders are picture and track film that is placed in the front and back of the reel. It's like the blank tape on both ends of an audio cassette.

The assistant editor may also have to find and pull **temp music** for the editor. This is especially common on low-budget films. Temp music is used to fill long patches of silence until the composer writes the real music for the sound track. It is usually pulled from classical compact disc recordings or other movie sound tracks.

RELATED JOBS:
Film editor
Sound effects editor

Sometimes Barbara's job is very hectic. "When they decide to have a surprise screening without notice, the pressure is on for you to get the film ready for projection. You have to check the reels to make sure everything is in **sync**," she explains. Sync is short for **synchronization**. In filmmaking, it means that the picture and the sound match perfectly.

In spite of the hectic moments, Barbara loves her job. She says that the best part is "the satisfaction of seeing all your hard work up on the screen when it's all over with." She is especially proud of the Disney films she has worked on. "These films will live on and entertain audiences for generations to come," she says proudly.

Have You Got What It Takes?

An assistant film editor has lots to do. You have to build select rolls. You have to create head and tail leaders, find temp music,

An assistant film editor checks a label on a piece of film.

and deal with film labs. And you have to keep track of everything. Whew!

Barbara worked her way up. "First, I worked at an independent production company as a gofer," she says. Gofers perform a lot of tasks, get last-minute props, return phone calls, help with crowd control. "It might not sound glamorous," Barbara says, "but it's a great learning position." Gofers and production assistants get to learn about all the different areas of film production. And that knowledge can help you get to where you want to be.

After working as a gofer for a while, Barbara decided she wanted to get into editing. "I was fascinated with the editing process, the **postproduction** end of filming," Barbara relates. "Film editors are the people who really put the movie together. And that's exciting."

An assistant film editor should be "cheery, organized, and neat," Barbara says. A positive attitude is important, because you'll be working with many different people—the director, the film editor, the **sound effects editor**, and lab technicians.

Organization is essential. Everything has to be recorded carefully. If something isn't documented, it could be lost forever and the final film could suffer!

An assistant film editor should also be a hard worker. "I work long hours," Barbara groans. "Some films require a lot of overtime, sometimes late into the evening." If you're not willing to put in the time and effort, then this job isn't for you.

Are you interested in becoming an assistant film editor? Go to the movies. We're not kidding! While you watch, notice how the scenes are put together. Think about what works, what doesn't, and why. You can do the same thing when you rent videos or watch films on TV.

It's also a good idea to learn how to operate a video camera. Once you are familiar with how the camera works, shoot everything in sight. Interview your family and friends. Have two people tell the same story and think about how you would edit each one to convey its special quality.

Barbara also recommends working your way up as she did. Try to get a job as a gofer or production assistant. Once you're working somewhere, offer to help out in any way you can. Editors are often overworked. They'll be glad to hand over some of their menial tasks. And you'll get to learn the ropes.

FILM EDITORS ARE THE PEOPLE WHO REALLY PUT THE MOVIE TOGETHER."

SOUND RECORDIST

Nuts and Bolts of the Job

You're shooting a movie on location in New York City. You've got crowds and traffic nearby, and a jet plane flying overhead. No matter how you set up the microphone, you still pick up city noise. But thanks to **ADR/Foley sound recordists** like Dean, the noise isn't a problem.

Why? Because Dean can record the voices and sounds later, in a recording studio. *Then* they're added to the film!

ADR (automated dialogue replacement) adds synchronized dialogue to a silent sound track. **Foley** does the same thing with sound effects, although sound effects have to be created first. We'll explain that in the Foley artist profile.

"The first thing I do every morning is check to make sure all the machines are working properly," Dean tells us. Then he cleans all the heads. Heads are the parts of a tape recorder that record or play back the magnetic symbols on a tape. "I use a cleaning solvent to wipe dust away," he explains. Next, using a screwdriver, Dean sets the recording levels on the recording machines.

When the **ADR/Foley mixer** arrives, he or she sets up the microphones. Then the mixer sets the levels on the **mixing console**. A mixing console is the master control unit in the recording studio. The mixer uses it to control desired sounds in a **mix**. When a person is being recorded, the sound goes from the microphone to the mixing console, and then from the mixing console to the tape.

RELATED JOBS:
ADR mixer
Camera assistant

During an ADR recording session, the actors

face a screen that shows the scene that is being rerecorded. With the help of headphones, they receive cues telling them when to speak their lines.

Meanwhile, Dean sits in the control room with the sound mixer. The mixer's job is to blend the sounds that come through the microphones. While he or she does this, Dean monitors the machines' meters carefully. He has to make sure that the dialogue is being recorded at the proper levels. The mixer and recordist work together to adjust levels so that the dialogue sounds perfect.

While recording, Dean keeps accurate logs of what or who is being recorded. He also labels and files the tapes for future use by the editors and mixers. "I create a road map for the editors and mixers. There are mountains of tapes, and they have to be able to find what they're looking for," he says.

ADR and Foley recording is usually done on digital multitrack tape or 4-track $1/4''$ tape. These are reel-to-reel tapes that can record up to 32 different channels of information. That means you can record 32 different sounds at once on a single reel of tape! That's why it's important for Dean to log and label everything carefully.

Dean's favorite part of the job is meeting the directors and stars of the films he works on. "I've had the chance to meet and work with Ridley Scott, who was very generous and gracious with his time. And when I worked on *Thelma and Louise*, I got to meet Susan Sarandon, who I have admired for many years," he relates.

"One of my most satisfying working experiences was on Madonna's *Truth or Dare*," Dean beams. "It was fun." Even though the film was a documentary, almost 90 percent of the film had to be "revoiced" with ADR recording to achieve a higher sound quality. "The best part was meeting Madonna. I was working day in and day out with her—sitting next to her—sharing soft drinks—she was almost a regular person!"

"I CREATE A ROAD MAP FOR THE EDITORS AND MIXERS."

Have You Got What It Takes?

Dean came out to Hollywood from Chicago. He had no definite plans, so he just floundered around, doing odd jobs in the industry. "I worked in many different temporary jobs in the film business," says Dean. "I worked in production as a production assistant and a **camera assistant**."

As a camera assistant, Dean was responsible for keeping track of things. He also learned how to set up the "road map" for editors and other postproduction people. This experience helped him land the job he has now. "I was able to get this job without having a lot of

A sound recordist cleans the heads on a sound mixer.

Two sound recordists make adjustments on the console.

sound experience. I was trained as an ADR/Foley sound recordist and ended up keeping the position," he says.

When Dean started working as an ADR/Foley sound recordist, his company was nonunion. Later, the local sound union stepped in to organize the company, and Dean was able to join. "This opened the opportunity for many different jobs," says Dean.

An ADR/Foley sound recordist "must be patient," Dean urges. You have to make sure that the machines are working well, and sometimes they break down. "Recording machines can be annoying at the worst times," Dean says.

You must also be detail-oriented to be a sound recordist. The log keeping and the "road mapping" are extremely important. "Poor record keeping will cause major problems down the line and will come back to haunt you," Dean says.

"RECORDING MACHINES CAN BE ANNOYING AT THE WORST TIMES."

A sound recordist must be a hard worker, too, because the hours get very long. "The bad part of the job is having to work until midnight with no warning," Dean complains. He usually starts at 8 A.M., so going to midnight makes a 15-hour day! But Dean, a union member, is compensated by being paid overtime.

And, of course, it helps if you love the movies. "The glamour goes away very quickly," says Dean. "You must have fun working on a movie or show, enjoy the process, or it gets boring very, very quickly." Recording can get tedious—sometimes you have to record a line of dialogue or a sound effect over and over again.

Are you interested in becoming a sound recordist? It's a good idea to learn how basic recording machines work. If you can get your hands on a high quality tape recorder with a mike, practice taping sounds and voices you hear. Experiment with different acoustics and volumes.

You can also join the sound crew at local or school theaters. Or offer to run the sound board at school dances. Working with machines and sounds at the same time will put you on the right path.

FOLEY ARTIST

Nuts and Bolts of the Job

The man on the screen enters his office. He places his briefcase on his desk ("rap!"). He puts his keys into his pocket ("clink-clink"). He sits down in his chair ("plop!"). He opens his squeaky top drawer ("kleeeeeee"). And then he pulls out a revolver, which accidentally goes off ("BAM!").

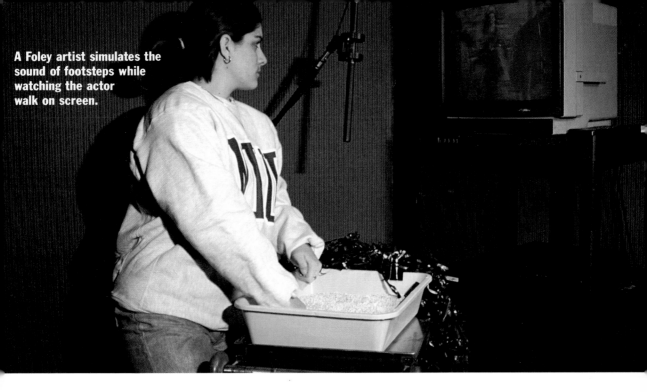

A Foley artist simulates the sound of footsteps while watching the actor walk on screen.

At the movies, the sounds match the actions on the screen. But sounds are often distorted during filming. So they are recreated *after* filming, in a stage called Foley.

Foley artists like Casey recreate these sound effects. Casey runs her own company in Burbank, California. She's been doing Foley for seven years.

Foley is the art of making sound effects for things like walking, running, and driving. "I replace footsteps and movements, and create sounds like paper shuffling and keys jingling," Casey explains. "The average viewer doesn't realize that sounds like this are *not* recorded during the filming process."

Casey's studio is set up for recording. But it also has a screen for viewing the scenes that need new sound effects. Casey works with a sound recordist (like Dean) and a sound mixer.

RELATED JOBS:
ADR/Foley mixer
ADR/Foley recordist

Like all Foley artists, Casey creates her sounds on a **Foley pit**. A Foley pit is a platform in a recording studio. It has various types of surfaces such as concrete, wood, and carpet. It also has a sandbox and other props that help create sound effects.

"The first thing I do is view the reel and listen," Casey says. A good Foley artist *listens* to the film instead of just watching it. He or she listens to what the actors are walking on and what the actors are picking up.

While Casey listens, she pays special attention to the surfaces she sees on the screen. She writes those surfaces down on **cue sheets**. Later, when she is actually recording, she uses the cue sheets to see exactly what kind of sound she has to create next. For example, if she has to imitate the sound of someone sliding across a car seat, she checks her cue sheet to see if it's a leather or a cloth seat. "You really have to match what's in the film," she says.

Casey works on ten-minute reels of film at a time. "Otherwise my brain starts going off in a hundred directions," she says. Casey usually does footsteps first for each reel. "I lay out my men's shoes, my high heels, and if someone wore slippers, I lay those out," she says.

Casey does footsteps while she watches and listens to the film. She tries to get her steps and the steps in the film to match as closely as possible. Meanwhile, the Foley recordist is taping the sounds she's making.

When the footsteps have been recorded, Casey works on sounds made with props. "I check my cue sheet and start laying out my props," she says. "I work with my mixer and my recordist. We work together to make the noise that's going to sound the best. It can get tricky because you don't use the real thing for the sound. Sometimes we use film reels and tennis shoes for bicycles. We put the two sounds together and they sound great," she tells us.

Sometimes Casey's company does special effects for things like monsters. Casey worked on Stephen King's *It*, which was an 18-foot spider! "We had to make sounds for breaking its legs and pulling out its heart!" Casey laughs. "I ended up using a crab body and a chicken body. I put the crab shell on top of the chicken. Then I pulled the legs off the crab, broke through the shell, and pulled out the chicken heart. It worked like a charm!"

Casey really loves being a Foley artist. "I consider myself lucky because I get to play in the sandbox all day," Casey laughs. "And I have a great time doing it." Casey's job allows her to be creative. And she uses her brain to come up with ways to make different sounds. She also gets to pretend she's different people. "I might play a big New York cop who just rescued 20 people or something. I find it a lot easier to be me because I get to play all these people," Casey admits.

Although Casey loves playing different characters, she says that "the best part of the job is when you review the reel and see what you've done. It's amazing to see all of it in sync. It sounds so good. The happiest time for a Foley artist is when they drop the music sound track in favor of your effects," she says.

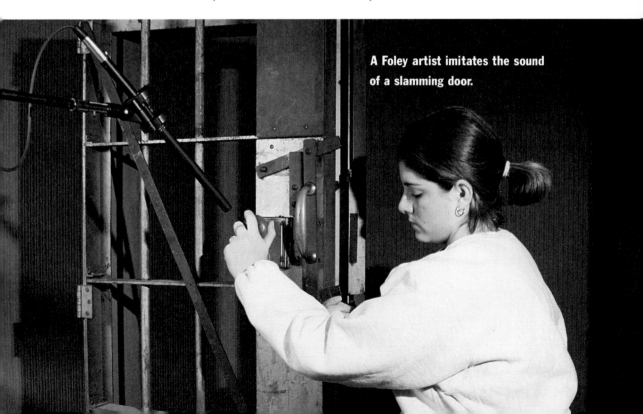

A Foley artist imitates the sound of a slamming door.

Have You Got What It Takes?

Casey grew up in Los Angeles, where her father was a Foley artist. As a kid, Casey hung out in the studio, watching her dad work. "My father told me that he thought I'd be good at Foley," Casey relates. So Casey decided to make a career out of sound effects.

A good Foley artist needs "a really good imagination, because you don't use the real thing for the sound you're trying to reproduce," she says. You have to figure out how to make noises that sound exactly like other noises.

Casey is always looking for and listening to new sounds. "Some people don't let me into their houses because I'm constantly picking up different objects to see what kinds of sounds they make!" Casey jokes.

A Foley artist also needs good timing. It's not easy to make footsteps and noises at exactly the right moment. "People either have the knack for Foley or they don't," Casey tells us. "Some people couldn't step Foley to save their lives. And that's just the way it is," she says.

"Most Foley artists are free-spirited—their personalities are wild and vibrant. You have to be a very 'out there' type...energetic...a go-getter," says Casey. You can't say things like "I don't have that prop" or "I can't do that." Instead you should ask, "What can I do to make it work?"

Foley artists also have to be flexible and willing to work long hours. ADR recording is usually done in the daytime to accommodate the talent. So Foley people have to do most of their work at night. "You start at seven and you may have to go to three o'clock in the morning," Casey says.

A FOLEY ARTIST NEEDS A GOOD IMAGINATION AND GOOD TIMING.

Are you interested in becoming a Foley artist? Casey suggests you find out where the soundstages are. But she admits that it's not easy to break into the field. "It's tough. You have to find a Foley artist who's willing to show you the ropes." Foley is an art form that's handed down from the professionals. There are no training schools for it.

Try to find someone like Casey. She has brought several people into Foley. "I have kid interns fairly regularly. I say, 'Come watch me!' I give the person a couple of things to do," she says.

If you think you've got what it takes to be a Foley artist, see what kinds of sounds different objects make. Watch TV and videos. Listen carefully for the sounds you hear on the screen. Notice everything. Then turn off the sound and try to recreate the sounds you don't hear!

OPTICAL EFFECTS TIMER

Nuts and Bolts of the Job

You're watching a movie, and there's a blizzard on the screen. Blinding snow falls in swirls, covering everything. You've never seen so much snow in your life. But this is a *movie*. The snowstorm is on film. How did they shoot during weather like this?

They didn't. The snow was added *after* the film was shot, on a large stage against a black background. Then it was placed over the original scene using an optical camera. The **superimposition** of the two images is called an optical effect.

Dan is an **optical effects timer**. It's his job to make sure that the snow looks real. The snow's color and density, or heaviness, has

An optical effects cameraperson loads film.

to match the original image very closely. Dan works hard to make sure that the optical effects in a movie don't stick out. "I have to make sure that the effect matches the rest of the film. It has to look natural," Dan says. "The point is to fool the audience into believing it's real."

Dan uses a machine called a **hazeltine** when he works. "When I use a hazeltine, I see the image on a monitor. As I adjust the color I can see the changes on the film. I can make very slight adjustments or big changes. If the negative permits, I can even make a daytime shot look like a night shot."

There are four basic optical effects: **fade-in, fade-out, dissolve**, and superimposition. A fade-in starts out black and gradually lightens

RELATED JOBS:
Optical
cameraperson
Film processor
Optical timer's
assistant

34

until we see the image on the screen. A fade-out is just the opposite—the scene fades away until we see a black screen.

A dissolve is a combination of a fade-in and a fade-out. It features one image fading in while another is fading out. In a superimposition, like the snowstorm, two images are on the screen at the same time.

After Dan times these optical effects, they are shot on film with an optical camera. The optical camera photographs the original image with the effect Dan wants. This creates a duplicate negative. "Creating a duplicate negative lets me try different things without worrying about damaging the original film."

Many optical effects involve a process in which a **matte shot** is made. This process puts different images together to make a third image that didn't exist to begin with. Using two mattes, Dan creates a brand new piece of film. He can combine a shot of an astronaut in

An optical effects timer at work on a hazeltine.

a studio with a lunar landscape to create an image of a man on the moon! And if he does his job right, the image looks like the real thing.

But where does Dan get a photograph of the moon? Filmmakers usually use film footage of the Nevada Desert or Death Valley. The film is stored in a **stock library**. This library is full of images that Dan's company will use again and again, images like deserts, mountains, snow, and rain. With Dan's magic **timing** ability, he can use this film to create very different effects!

With each movie, Dan has to keep in contact with many different people on the project. "You have to be a good listener. Sometimes the director wants a certain mood, and sometimes the director of photography wants a certain look. You have to be able to figure out exactly what they want." This part of the job is not always easy.

Dan's job can also be tough when there's a shift in film color at the lab. A client might not understand the technical aspects involved in Dan's work. "I have to convince them that the color problem is in the print, not in the optical negative," Dan says. Sometimes a client just doesn't believe that the optical will work. Dan has to be patient with the client and the process. Combining optical effects takes a lot of hard work.

In spite of the hard parts, Dan enjoys his work. "The best part is being creative," Dan says. "And the challenge. It's great when the client says go ahead and do what *you* think will work."

Have You Got What It Takes?

Surprisingly, Dan wasn't set on a career in the movies. "I was never really into the movies," he says. "I was into sports and baseball."

After high school, he got a job in the shipping department at Technicolor. "I started out at Technicolor in shipping. I did small tasks like packing and logging shipments," Dan recalls. Later Dan moved to another shipping job at a company called Movie Lab.

After working at Movie Lab for a while, Dan heard about a job opening for an **optical timer's assistant**. "They needed someone to take notes for the timer. I went to viewings in dark screening rooms and wrote down what people said—what had to be done to the film. I worked for the timers for about two or three years," Dan tells us.

"THE POINT IS TO FOOL THE AUDIENCE INTO BELIEVING IT'S REAL."

From there, Dan got a job as a timer. He made sure that the **dailies**—the reels of film shot each day—looked like the rest of the film for the movie. "Now I'm doing optical effects timing for the movies," he says.

An optical effects timer should be a good listener. "You have to listen carefully to what the client wants," Dan says. "There are many ways to do optical effects. But you have to please the person you're working for."

You also have to be patient. "Combining several pieces of film takes a lot of time and work," Dan says. The final product has to look good. "Optical effects scenes that are not well done look grainy or darker than the rest of the film," explains Dan.

Optical effects timing is not taught in schools. You can't learn how to do it by reading a book. Like most jobs in the movies, it has to be learned on the job. But if you're determined, you can get into this field.

Start by learning about photography. You'll learn about film and the different kinds of processing. You can also try to get a job in a photo lab. Start out with an entry-level position as Dan did. While you work, watch what's going on around you. Ask questions. This tactic worked for Dan.

FOUR THINGS TO REMEMBER NO MATTER WHAT FILM JOB YOU WANT

1. Do your homework.

Find out what kinds of jobs are available. Use the library. If you're in school, ask your guidance counselor about internships or jobs in film. He or she might know about programs that are right for you.

If you're in a small town, call the chamber of commerce and ask if there are any local film studios. If you're near a major city, get in touch with a motion picture studio. You can even look in the yellow pages under "Motion Pictures—Production Companies."

2. Get yourself out there.

Once you get in touch with these studios, ask if they have any entry-level positions. Find out what the qualifications are. If you're told there's nothing for you, ask if they're interested in taking an intern for free. No-cost labor can be hard for a studio to resist.

Next, get a résumé ready. A résumé should include your name, address, and phone number; your goal; your level of schooling and the schools you attended; your work history; your extracurricular activities in school, such as soccer team, film club, or makeup for the school plays; any helpful skills, like typing, languages, computers, or mastery of your family's camcorder; any personal interests and hobbies that might relate to the film industry.

If you're mailing in a résumé, include a short letter telling why you're interested in working at that studio. Let the organization you're writing to know when you're available. Explain that you're excited about any work that might be available.

A sample résumé appears at the end of this chapter.

Always look and act your best at interviews. Be alert, energetic, and excited about your chosen career. If you really want a job in film, show it. Make your feelings known. Even if you have to start at the bottom of the ladder, be gracious and eager.

3. Find a mentor.

Don't be afraid to ask questions. That's the only way you're going to learn the answers! Befriend an experienced co-worker. Look upon that friend as your mentor or teacher, your stepping stone to the next level of advancement. Or you may find a friend or relative who can help you get your first job in film.

Always remember people who have helped you along the way. These people are special. They did not have to take time away from their work to show you the ropes. They did it because they liked and respected you. And don't forget that you are a member of a team. One person alone can't make a film. It takes hundreds of dedicated people!

4. Work your way up.

Be prepared to work hard for little or no money in the beginning. The important thing is to get experience. That experience will help you get the job you want later.

Keep your ultimate goal in mind. Focus on your reward even during the tough times. And remember that even if you're working as a gofer or a production assistant, you're still part of the team. You're part of the filmmaking process. Someday you just might see your name in credits on the big screen!

A career in film is not for everybody. It's only for those who share a passion for movies. Films are magical, and the people who make them are wizards and magicians—from the gofer to the director. Without all the players, there would be no movies. It's up to you now. So get ready to hear—*lights, camera, action!*

Jane Warner
2222 Sunset Boulevard
Los Angeles, CA 90046
(213) 555-1234

OBJECTIVE	Internship or entry-level position in film production.
EDUCATION	Erie High School, Toledo, Ohio Expect to graduate June 1995
WORK EXPERIENCE	Counselor, Akron YMCA Camp, Akron, Ohio Full-time, 6/92 to 9/92. Supervised 10- through 12-year-old campers, taught soccer to all campers, drove school bus. Cashier, Burgers 'R' Us, Toledo, Ohio Part-time, 9/91 to 6/93. Advised customers, operated cash register, cooked and prepared food.
SKILLS	Knowledge of home video equipment Conversational Spanish Computer, word processing, typing
ACTIVITIES	Junior varsity soccer team, 2 years Spanish Club, 4 years Computer Users Group, 2 years
INTERESTS	Home video making, foreign cars, in-line skating, mountain biking

GLOSSARY

ADR (automated dialogue replacement) The process of adding synchronized dialogue to a silent sound track. After the filming, the performer's voice is taped in a recording studio.

ADR/Foley mixer A person who mixes onto one tape the sounds recorded during an ADR session.

ADR/Foley sound recordist A person who operates the recording machines during an ADR recording session.

animation The technique of using drawn characters and making them appear life-like on the screen.

assistant film editor A person who assists the film editor.

best boy The gaffer's assistant.

camera assistant A person who assists with cameras on the set, doing tasks like loading and keeping track of film.

coding machine A machine that stamps matching numbers at regular intervals on the film footage.

creature designer A person who creates nonhuman creatures for film.

cue sheets A log designating when pieces of sound footages begin and end. Cue sheets are used in ADR and Foley recording.

dailies A print of the film that was shot on the previous day; also called **rushes.**

director of photography (DP) A person who designs and oversees the lighting of a film. The DP chooses camera lenses and supervises camera movement.

dissolve A visual effect on film in which one image fades in while another fades out.

fade-in A visual effect in which the screen starts out black and gradually lightens until an image can be seen.

fade-out A visual effect in which a scene fades away until the screen is completely black.

film editor A person who cuts and splices film stock to create a movie.

film processor A person in a photo lab who processes the film.

flatbed or **moviola** A machine that allows an editor to view the picture and sound tracks at different speeds.

Foley The process of creating sound effects to match the actions on the film.

Foley artist A person who creates sound effects, such as footsteps.

Foley pit A platform in a recording studio where a Foley artist works. Foley pits have various surfaces and props that are used to create sound effects.

gaffer The chief electrical lighting technician on the set.

gofer A person who performs menial tasks, offering general help in a film studio.

grip A person responsible for putting up sets and for rigging lights and cameras.

hazeltine A machine that allows an optical effects person to make adjustments to the film.

independent production company A production company that is not associated with a major movie studio.

key grip The grip in charge. Grips are responsible for putting up sets and for rigging lights and cameras.

lamp operator A person who is responsible for operating lights on the set.

leaders Film that is added to the beginning and the end of a reel.

location The place, away from a studio lot, where the shooting of a film takes place.

location driver A person who transports sets, lights, and lighting equipment. Location drivers may also transport talent.

makeup assistant A person who helps the film's makeup artist.

matte shot A piece of film footage that is created by combining parts of two other pieces of footage.

mix (mixing) The blending of two or more signals on the multi-sound track or tracks.

mixing console A master unit used to control sounds in a recording studio.

optical cameraperson A person who operates the camera when shooting or creating special visual effects.

optical effects timer A person who controls the color and density of film footage with optical effects.

optical timer's assistant A person who assists the optical effects timer.

postproduction The work done on a film after the actual filming (production) takes place. This is when editing, ADR, Foley, and timing, scoring, and other processes begin.

prerig To place electric cable where you think lights might be used before actually rigging the lights.

production assistant An entry-level position in the film industry. Production assistants offer general production help.

select rolls Rolls of film footage that contain only the select takes.

select takes Takes from a shoot that the director considers the best.

set carpenter A person who builds scenery for a set and/or does general handiwork on the set.

sound effects editor A person who decides what sound effects to add to a film. A sound effects editor may also record and synchronize the effects in a film.

special effects coordinator A person who oversees and coordinates the special effects in a film.

special effects makeup artist A person who uses cosmetics to make an actor look like a monster or other creature.

stock library A collection of film with different images on it, such as snow, rain, sunshine.

superimposition A visual effect in which one image is imposed on top of another image so that both are visible on the screen.

sync (synchronization) The positioning of a sound track so that the sound matches the actions on film.

talent Performers in a film.

teamster driver A person who picks up and delivers packages containing such things as film reels, scripts, and soundtracks.

temp music Music that is used temporarily to fill in long patches of silence in a film until the composer writes the actual music.

timing The process of selecting the proper light and color balance for each scene.

trims A piece of film stock that is left over after a portion of that take has been cut out and used in the making of the film.

union A group of workers that join together to protect the wages and working conditions of the organization's members.

INDEX